Baltimore Bride's Quilt Designs

Doreen Lynn Saunders

DOVER PUBLICATIONS, INC.
NEW YORK

Copyright © 1993 by Dover Publications, Inc.
All rights reserved under Pan American and International Copyright Conventions.

Published in Canada by General Publishing Company, Ltd., 30 Lesmill Road, Don Mills, Toronto, Ontario.
Published in the United Kingdom by Constable and Company, Ltd., 3 The Lanchesters, 162–164 Fulham Palace Road, London W6 9ER.

Baltimore Bride's Quilt Designs is a new work, first published by Dover Publications, Inc., in 1993.

DOVER *Pictorial Archive* SERIES

This book belongs to the Dover Pictorial Archive Series. You may use the designs and illustrations for graphics and crafts applications, free and without special permission, provided that you include no more than four in the same publication or project. (For permission for additional use, please write to Dover Publications, Inc., 31 East 2nd Street, Mineola, N.Y. 11501.)

However, republication or reproduction of any illustration by any other graphic service, whether it be in a book or in any other design resource, is strictly prohibited.

Library of Congress Cataloging-in-Publication Data

Saunders, Doreen Lynn.
    Baltimore bride's quilt designs / Doreen Lynn Saunders.
       p.   cm. — (Dover pictorial archive series)
    ISBN 0-486-27610-4 (pbk.)
    1. Appliqué — Patterns. 2. Album quilts — Maryland — Baltimore. 3. Patchwork—Patterns. I. Title. II. Series.
TT779.S28   1993
745.4—dc20
                                                                                          93-10728
                                                                                              CIP

Manufactured in the United States of America
Dover Publications, Inc., 31 East 2nd Street, Mineola, N.Y. 11501

INTRODUCTION

The appliquéd album quilt plays an important and extremely decorative role in America's quiltmaking tradition. Unlike the typical patchwork quilt, where one or two identical blocks are repeated over and over, each block in an album quilt is different. A wide variety of elaborate motifs appeared in the blocks—birds, animals, ships, historic buildings, patriotic emblems and a profusion of plants and flowers—and bright, primary colors predominated, contrasting strongly with the white background.

Album quilts were generally made as gifts, and often (although not always), each block was contributed by a different friend or relative of the recipient. This style of quilt flourished in the mid-nineteenth century, with several types being popular—friendship quilts, autograph quilts, presentation quilts and, of course, bride's quilts.

Today, the album quilts made in Baltimore during the 1840s and 1850s are particularly prized. It is apparent that competition among the ladies of the city resulted in a high degree of artistry and skill with the needle, and the imaginative designs, superb color sense and exquisite workmanship have made Baltimore Album Quilts the standard for this style of quiltmaking.

Because of the intricacy of the blocks and the high quality of the designs in the Baltimore quilts, and because of similarities from quilt to quilt, it is now believed that a group of professional quiltmakers sold designs for blocks as well as actual blocks for inclusion in these quilts.

In these pages, you will find a beautiful collection of floral blocks and borders adapted from Baltimore Bride's Quilts and other Baltimore Album Quilts. There are more than enough motifs here to inspire you to create a whole gardenful of one-of-a-kind album quilts.

3

9

19

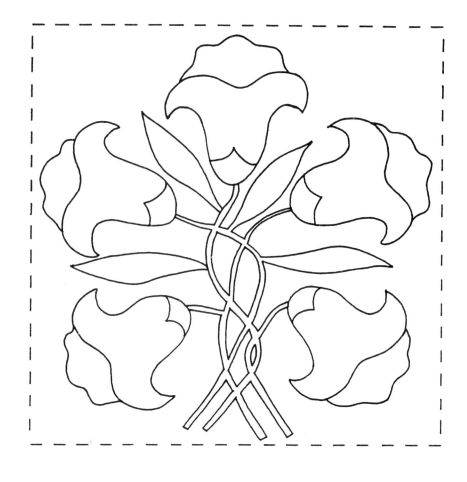